see
& eat

Sweet Potato

Carmel Houston-Price, Bethany Chapman, Katrina Dulay,
Natalie Ellison, Kate Harvey, Natalie Masento and David Messer

Published by the University of Reading, Reading, UK
Copyright © University of Reading

ISBN: 978-0-7049159-8-5

SEE & EAT is a trademark.

Design by Fuzzy Flamingo
www.fuzzyflamingo.co.uk

Images used under license from Shutterstock.com

The story of 🌱 see & eat

The SEE & EAT team are passionate about helping little ones to know and love their vegetables!

We know it can be difficult for parents to persuade young children to eat a variety of vegetables and we have been working hard on ways to make this easier. Research led by Professor Carmel Houston-Price at the University of Reading has shown that pre-schoolers are more likely to eat vegetables at mealtimes if they are already familiar with how the vegetable looks and where it comes from. The more familiar your child is with a food before it appears on their plate, the better… and this is especially true for vegetables they don't like or haven't tried before!

SEE & EAT books are an easy, effective and fun way to introduce children to vegetables before they try them.

SEE & EAT books help children to get to know their vegetables by showing each food's journey 'from farm to fork'. Our research shows that looking at a SEE & EAT picture book with your child for a few minutes each day for a couple of weeks is enough to make a difference. After looking at one of our books, children are often more willing to taste the vegetable than they were beforehand. They eat more of it, and seem to enjoy eating it more, too!

For more information about the research behind SEE & EAT, visit our website at www.research.reading.ac.uk/kids-food-choices

How to use this book to help your little one to know and love sweet potato!

- Look at this book about sweet potato with your child for a few minutes every day for a couple of weeks.
- Make reading time fun! Find a time and place to look at the book each day that works best for you and your child. Feel free to look at the sweet potato book in your own way. You might want to talk about the different shapes and sizes of sweet potatoes, whether you have ever grown or picked sweet potatoes yourself, where you usually buy them, or how you like to prepare and eat them. Always be positive about sweet potatoes!
- After two weeks, go shopping for sweet potato with your child, if you can. Point out sweet potatoes in the shop and involve your child in preparing the sweet potatoes back at home. You might want to try our simple recipes at the end of this book. Then, serve them up. It's time to find out whether your child will swallow up their sweet potato!
- Remember to chop vegetables into small pieces and to keep an eye on your little ones while they are eating, especially if they are just starting to eat solid foods or the vegetable is new to them.
- Even if they taste just a tiny piece, that is a great start. Don't worry if they refuse to eat it, keep on offering sweet potato at mealtimes and they are likely to accept it in the end.
- Then it's time to choose another of our vegetable books so that your little one can learn to love another vegetable!

These are sweet potatoes.

They have pinky-red or brown skin and are usually orange on the inside.

But did you know that some sweet potatoes are white inside?

Sweet potatoes are large roots that we can eat.

Sweet potatoes grow underground, so they are mostly hidden by the earth while they are growing.

But we can see the green trailing stems and leaves of the sweet potatoes while they are growing.

They need lots of space and warm sunny weather to grow.

Time to dig up the sweet potatoes...

… and pull them out!

Sweet potatoes can have pointy ends or round ends and can grow to different sizes.

You can buy sweet potatoes at the market or in a supermarket.

You can cook them whole, like a baked potato, with their skin on...

...or you can peel them before you cut them into pieces.

Sweet potatoes taste very sweet if they are roasted until they are soft and brown.

Sweet potatoes are tasty when you have them as fries or in soup.

We like to eat roast sweet
potatoes with their skins on!

How do YOU like
to eat them?

More ideas to help your child to know and love their vegetables!

- Take your child to a farm shop or farmer's market or look out for open days at local farms.
- In the supermarket, let your child find and choose the sweet potatoes for you, and point out their different sizes and shapes and the colours of their skins.
- Encourage your child to explore the look, smell and feel of sweet potatoes by hiding them amongst other vegetables in a bag and playing a guessing game to see if your child can identify them by touch, smell or hearing you describe them.
- Let your child be your little helper in the kitchen. Choose a simple recipe and talk through the steps. Children can help wash the sweet potatoes, put ingredients in a bowl or pass you utensils.
- Make up sweet potato songs to sing with your child.
- Try to ensure that vegetables cover one third of the plate so that your child learns what a healthy plate looks like.
- And remember… it is a good idea to eat together as a family if you can, even if this is just one meal at the weekend. It could be at breakfast, lunch or dinnertime – whatever works best for your family.
- Visit our website (www.seeandeat.org) for more activities and games and to download SEE & EAT ebooks.

Simple suggestions for preparing sweet potatoes

Sweet potato fries

1. Chop the sweet potato into thin strips. If you wash them first, there's no need to peel them.
2. Toss the sweet potato strips in a small amount of flour, then toss them in oil.
3. Season them with a small amount of salt and pepper.
4. Spread the sweet potato strips on a baking tray and bake them at 200°C for about 20mins. Shake the tray at regular intervals to move the sweet potatoes around.

Sweet potato mash

1. Peel and chop the sweet potato into large pieces.
2. Simmer the pieces in a saucepan for about 15 mins, checking they are cooked by prodding them with a fork.
3. Drain and mash the sweet potato with a dash of milk to soften it all up. Sweet potatoes take less time to cook than other potatoes and need less liquid to make mash.
4. Serve as a side dish instead of traditional mashed potato.

We would love to hear how you get on with the SEE & EAT books and activities.

Share your stories with us by emailing us at SeeAndEat@reading.ac.uk

or by contacting the project lead,
Professor Carmel Houston-Price
School of Psychology & Clinical Language Sciences,
University of Reading,
Earley Gate,
Whiteknights,
Reading, UK
RG6 6ES

Acknowledgements

The SEE & EAT team at the University of Reading are indebted to the hundreds of children, parents, teachers and healthcare professionals who have taken part in the research studies, workshops and focus groups that have helped us make SEE & EAT activities as effective as they can be.

We are grateful to EIT Food for funding the work of the SEE & EAT team since 2019. EIT Food is the innovation community for Food of the European Institute of Innovation and Technology (EIT), a body of the EU under Horizon 2020, the EU Framework Programme for Research and Innovation.

We are also grateful to our partners at the Open University, the Universities of Turin, Warsaw and Helsinki, British Nutrition Foundation (BNF) and the European Food Information Council (EUFIC), who have helped to bring SEE & EAT activities to families across Europe.

Finally, we would like to thank Jen Parker at Fuzzy Flamingo (www.fuzzyflamingo.co.uk) for her support with the design and publication of this series of books and Sascha Landskron at Boom House Books (www.boomhousebooks.co.uk) for her enthusiasm for the SEE & EAT project, and for her support with marketing and promotion.

– Professor Carmel Houston-Price & the SEE & EAT team (Dr Bethany Chapman, Lily Clark, Dr Katrina May Dulay, Natalie Ellison, Professor Kate Harvey, Dr Sun Ae Kim, Dr Natalie Masento, Professor David Messer, Dr Alan Roberts)

 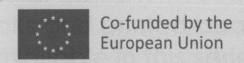 

Look out for the other books in the SEE & EAT series …

see
& eat

Helping your little ones
to know and love
their vegetables

Lettuce

see
& eat

Helping your little ones
to know and love
their vegetables

Peas

see ..... & eat

Helping your little ones to know and love their vegetables

Peppers

see ..... & eat

Helping your little ones to know and love their vegetables

Spinach

… and many more. Visit www.seeandeat.org for the library of ebooks and printed books that are now available in this series.